= Primary Sources of American Treaties™ =

The Treaty of Canandaigua, 1794

A Primary Source Examination of the Treaty
Between the United States and the
Tribes of Indians Called the Six Nations

ഈ ഈ ഈ

M. G. Mateusz

rosen central
Primary Source™

The Rosen Publishing Group, Inc., New York

made and concluded on the Eleventh day of November

Chiefs and Warriors of the Six Nations on the othe

For Nick

HHA

Published in 2006 by The Rosen Publishing Group, Inc.
29 East 21st Street, New York, NY 10010

Library of Congress Cataloging-in-Publication Data

Mateusz, M. G.
The Treaty of Canandaigua, 1794: a primary source examination of the treaty between the United States and the tribes of Indians called the Six Nations / M.G. Mateusz.—1st ed.
    p. cm.—(Primary sources of American treaties)
Includes bibliographical references and index.
ISBN 1-4042-0443-1 (library binding)
1. Iroquois Indians—Treaties. 2. Iroquois Indians—Land tenure. 3. Six Nations.
Treaties, etc. United States, 1794 Nov. 11. 4. Iroquois Indians—Government relations.
I. Title. II. Series.
KF8228.I76M38 2006
323.1197'55073—dc22

                                                                    2005003652

Manufactured in the United States of America

On the cover: Detail of George Caitlin's painting, *Portage Around the Falls of Niagara at Table Rock*, dated 1847–1848.

Contents

Introduction

On November 1794, a remarkable document was signed: the Treaty of Canandaigua. With this treaty, the United States government embarked on a new relationship with Native Americans. This meant that the government recognized the Indian nations as sovereign or independent nations, just like the United States, Great Britain, or France. The treaty also marked the first time the United States government tried a different approach when dealing with the Indian groups over the issue of land ownership.

By the late eighteenth century, the question of land was foremost in the minds of the new national government. Increasing numbers of people were moving farther west— many were relocating onto lands that were occupied and were in fact owned by several different Indian groups. Before the Treaty of Canandaigua, the United States relied on military threats or the use of treaties as a means of taking land away from Indians. In the majority of these cases, tribal claims or ownership rights to their lands were simply dismissed. As a result, Indians were often forced to move farther west.

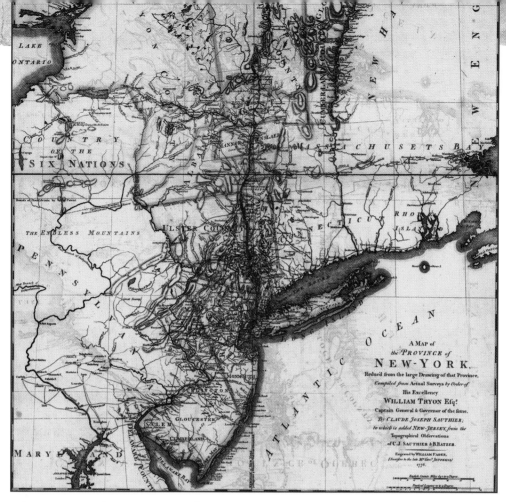

This engraved map dating from 1776 shows what, at the time, was called the Province of New York. The map also indicates where the various Native American tribes, such as the Six Nations, were concentrated in this part of the country. The map was created from a land survey that took place on behalf of His Excellency William Tryon, Esquire.

With the Treaty of Canandaigua (also sometimes known as the Treaty with the Six Nations), the United States government was finally able to realize two important goals. First, the government was able to achieve a formal peace with the Six Nations of the Iroquois Confederacy and the surrender of their claims to the Ohio Valley. Second, the government formally returned a large portion of land to the Senecas, one of the nations. This portion of land had been taken away from them a decade earlier with the Treaty of Fort Stanwix. Under the terms of the Treaty of Canandaigua, the United States government had a chance to control the Ohio Valley territory. At least for the time being, the treaty also ended any threat of war with the Six Nations. The federal government knew that such a war could be disastrous.

For the tribes of the Six Nations, the Treaty of Canandaigua was important because it formally defined their relationship with the American government. One particular article in the treaty—Article VII—makes clear the special status that the Six Nations enjoyed as independent nations with their own governments. This recognition has stood the test of time well into the twenty-first century, and in particular, with regard to land rights and the question of taxation for the members of the Six Nations.

Despite the treaty's tone of compromise and agreement, it was clear that the United States government would never stop its ongoing quest to expand its borders. The 1794 treaty was the result of the federal government's realization that a change of policy was desperately needed in order to achieve its goals while maintaining a lasting peace. In the end, the Treaty of Canandaigua did not ultimately prevent the United States from moving farther west or from taking away land that belonged to Indians. What it did do, however, was offer a way—at least temporarily—for both white Americans and Indians to settle their differences and recognize each other as equals.

1

The Struggle to Survive

Throughout the early decades of the eighteenth century, relations between English colonists and Indians remained fairly peaceful. However, many Indians watched uneasily as white settlers pushed westward in their endless quest for land. To complicate matters, the Indian groups in eastern North America were often as suspicious of each other as they were of whites. As a result, these groups were unable or unwilling to come together, even in the interest of protecting themselves from the invasion of their lands.

ᗨ A Tense Relationship ᗨ

By the late eighteenth century, Indian tribes in North America were struggling. Frequently and against their will, they had been drawn into a number of colonial wars as well as smaller conflicts involving the various European powers that had come to America. Since the establishment of Jamestown, Virginia, in 1607 (the first permanent English settlement in North America), Indians had found themselves fighting against the English, French, Dutch, and Spanish. In

As a result of the arrival of the English, French, Dutch, and Spanish, the Indian tribes were subjected to many germs and illnesses that were foreign to them. In particular, the smallpox virus was extremely devastating. The image at right depicts an Indian suffering from smallpox.

almost all of these cases, they sided with whomever promised to stay off their land and to protect them from the encroachment of others.

As a result of these various conflicts, Indian tribes, particularly those living along the eastern seaboard, endured horrible losses. In many cases, not only did they lose their homes and villages, but many also died due to war, disease, and starvation. Whereas once Indians had been in the majority, more white Europeans were now present on the land. To many European settlers, this was good news. It seemed that Indians were becoming less threatening to colonial settlements. However, Indians sensed that they were losing control of their fate and future.

⸗ The Six Nations ⸗

In the midst of these troubles, some Indian groups did develop the strength to resist whites. One of the most powerful and important of these groups was the Six Nations, more commonly known as the Iroquois Confederacy. The confederacy was made up of six distinct but related Indian nations: the

Mohawks, the Oneidas, the Onondagas, the Cayugas, the Senecas, and the Tuscaroras. All had settled in northeastern North America, mostly in the Finger Lakes and Mohawk Valley in western and central New York. Their lands extended from the Hudson River to the Genesee River. United by language and customs, these groups formed a powerful political and military union that dominated this region for more than two centuries.

For almost 125 years, the Iroquois Confederacy controlled this very important piece of territory. As a result, the Iroquois were often more powerful than the Europeans who settled there. Unlike the Iroquois Confederacy, the European settlers were divided and often at war with one another. They could not always unite against the Indians if the need to do so arose. As a result, for a time, the Iroquois Confederacy was the most powerful political body in the Northeast.

The Dutch, French, and English realized that, at the very least, the Iroquois Confederacy was the most important group of Indians with whom they had to deal. This was because the Iroquois held the key to the balance of power in North America. The Europeans also realized that they needed the Iroquois as trading partners. As such, the Europeans were more than willing to make the necessary agreements in exchange for the Iroquois' cooperation and access to their lands. This was especially so if such agreements prevented their colonial rivals from enjoying similar benefits. By maintaining unity and following a policy of playing one European power against the others, the Iroquois successfully controlled the Europeans for many years.

This is a rendition of what an Iroquois village looked like. The image is a part of a map of French Canada that was published in 1720. The village is surrounded by a tall fence (the technical term is a palisaded village) in order to keep enemy tribes out. In particular, the fierce warriors of the Algonquin tribe posed a threat to the Iroquois.

Of all the nations, the Iroquois Confederacy was the most successful at handling the problems that came about as a result of European settlement. Few other native peoples enjoyed the relative political, economic, and military self-sufficiency of the confederacy. Because of their strength and independence, the Iroquois presented a continual source of frustration to white expansion.

⌐ Covenant Chains ⌐

In 1677, the Iroquois further cemented their position as the dominant force in the Northeast with a series of treaties made with the British. Known as Covenant Chains, these treaties declared the Iroquois to be the leaders of all native peoples in most of present-day New York and Pennsylvania. The

This drawing from 1570 illustrates the legend of the formation of the Iroquois Confederacy. At right is the Onondaga sorcerer (with snakes in his hair) who refused to allow an end to the conflicts among the Iroquois tribes. However, the peacemakers Atortaro and Hiawatha (left) prevailed upon the sorcerer, thereby establishing peace.

agreements not only allowed the Iroquois Confederacy to maintain its power but also allowed other Indian groups in the region to trade more easily with the British and the Iroquois.

These treaties were settled through meetings between the colonial governor of New York and the Iroquois *sachems*, or leaders. Even though large numbers of Indians were present at these meetings, it was the sachems who spoke on behalf of their people. In this way, the English colonists maintained peaceful and prosperous relations with the Indians. Sometimes, however, the English demanded land from the Iroquois. To comply, the Iroquois gave the English land belonging to other Indian nations, such as the Shawnee and Delaware. Those tribes had fallen under the domination of the Iroquois.

⚊ Defeat ⚊

During the second half of the eighteenth century, the Iroquois found themselves caught in the middle as tensions grew between the French and British. By the time of the Seven Years' War in 1756, the Iroquois had become the unwilling allies of the British. Accordingly, they helped the Iroquois defeat the French in 1763. In 1776, the Iroquois again found themselves involved in another conflict—this time between the American colonists and the British government.

During the American Revolution (1775–1781), the once powerful Iroquois Confederacy began to crumble. The tribes divided among themselves—the Oneidas and Tuscaroras supported the Americans, while the remaining tribes of the confederacy supported the British. In 1779, near present-day Elmira, New York, the Iroquois suffered a terrible defeat at the hands of the Americans. Not more than two years later, the Iroquois suffered another blow when their British allies surrendered to the Americans. Clearly, the Iroquois Confederacy could no longer rely on the Covenant Chains with the British. Faced with a new and uncertain future, they wondered what further troubles awaited them.

2

The Drive for Land

On September 3, 1783, delegates, or government representatives, from Great Britain and the United States met to sign the Treaty of Paris. This meant a formal end to the war between the two countries and recognition of the independence of the United States. Among the many provisions of the treaty was the cessation, or giving up, of British ownership of all of the territory between the Allegheny Mountains and the Mississippi River. This doubled the size of the new United States. In making this agreement, neither side thought to consult the people who lived on the land. For the Americans, it was very important to find ways to settle and govern this territory, and to deal with the growing Native American hostilities.

⤝ Creating an Indian Policy ⤝

Shortly after ratifying, or passing, the Treaty of Paris, the American government created a special committee to deal more specifically with the settlement of the western territory and the resettlement of the Indians who lived there. In October 1783, the Committee on Indian Affairs of the

Continental Congress issued its first report. It recommended the creation of a boundary line between the United States and Indian territory as a way to avoid conflict. Another problem rose; the Treaty of Paris contained no provision for dealing with the Indians, especially those members of the Iroquois Confederacy who had sided with the British. Since representatives of the confederacy were not present at the treaty talks, the United States was still technically at war with them. The American government wanted to end hostilities with the Indians, particularly the Iroquois Confederacy. As a condition of peace *and* as punishment for siding with the British during the Revolution, the Americans insisted that the Iroquois cede a portion of their ancestral land to the United States.

-The Treaty of Fort Stanwix-

In March 1784, Congress elected a group of five men (including former Revolutionary War heroes George Rogers Clark and Nathaniel Greene) to act as commissioners in all treaty negotiations with the Six Nations. In October, formal treaty negotiations began between the representatives of the United States government and the Six Nations.

On October 22, 1784, delegates signed the Treaty of Fort Stanwix. The terms of the treaty stated that four tribes within the Iroquois Confederacy—the Senecas, Cayugas, Onondagas, and Mohawks—were to be treated as defeated nations and were thus subject to terms imposed by the American government. The treaty ordered the four tribes to turn over any American captives they still held. The defeated tribes also had

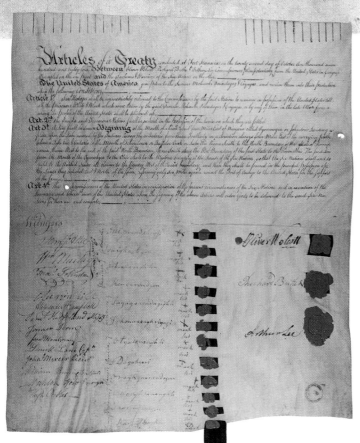

The Treaty of Fort Stanwix is pictured at left, complete with the wax seals of those who signed it. At the time, wax seals were used to authenticate important letters and documents. It used to be common practice to destroy a seal once the owner had died. For a partial transcription, see page 56.

to give up their claims to the Ohio Valley. The boundaries of this region—running south from a point approximately four miles (six kilometers) east of the Niagara River mouth to the northern boundary of Pennsylvania—included an area that presently makes up about one-fourth of the state of Pennsylvania. This provision took most of the land the Senecas had. However, the Six Nations held on to the lands east and north of the borders of New York and Pennsylvania. In addition, the two tribes that had supported the Americans during the war—the Tuscaroras and the Oneidas—maintained control over the lands on which they had settled. The representatives of the Six Nations were angered by the treaty, but they were intimidated by the presence of American troops. Forced to endure the aggressive tactics and disrespectful conduct of the American delegation, the Indians had little choice but to yield.

⸺ Backlash ⸺

The Treaty of Fort Stanwix formally ended the war between the United States of America and the Iroquois Confederacy. However, the treaty was unfair and did not bring equal benefits to both sides. This proved to be its undoing. In reality, the United States government had imposed a settlement upon the Indians as opposed to negotiating one. The tribes that had supported the British claimed they had never been defeated and that they had not surrendered. Thus, the government of the United States had no ground to treat them as a defeated enemy. However, because they no longer had the support of the British, there was little the Indians could do to defend their rights or their sovereignty. They believed the British had betrayed them when they gave the Americans land that did not belong to them. Instead, this land belonged to the Indians.

Outraged members of the Six Nations refused to ratify the Treaty of Fort Stanwix. Their protests were fruitless. As far as the United States government was concerned, the treaty was valid and would be enforced. This treaty also marked the first time that the United States government applied the principle of "conquest by treaty," in which Native American land was taken away through treaty negotiations. In the years to come, this practice became the basis of American negotiations with the Indians.

⸺The Treaty of Fort McIntosh ⸺

In 1785, Congress sent another group of commissioners to the Ohio Valley to negotiate another treaty with the Delaware,

Wyandot, Ottawa, and Chippewa Indians. Negotiations took place at Fort McIntosh, located in western Pennsylvania. In December 1784, accompanied by more than 400 warriors, leaders of the Ohio Valley tribes had traveled to the fort to meet the American commissioners. Most of the Indian representatives were younger chiefs who did not have the authority within their tribes to negotiate a treaty. Despite this problem, the American commissioners insisted that discussions proceed.

The Treaty of Fort McIntosh was signed on January 21, 1785. Similar to the terms of the Treaty of Fort Stanwix, the terms of this treaty were not so much agreed upon as imposed by the American government. Under the terms, the tribal leaders agreed that their people no longer constituted independent nations. Instead, they were under the jurisdiction of the United States. As well, the treaty forced the Indians to give up their lands in southern and eastern Ohio and to resettle in the western corner of present-day Ohio. The American officials promised that they would prevent squatters from encroaching on Indian lands, which, as it turned out, they failed to do.

When news of the terms reached the tribes, they were angry and in a state of disbelief. Most rejected the treaty—especially the Shawnees—who by now had lost all of their lands in southwestern Ohio. The Indians pointed out that the chiefs who had negotiated and signed the treaty did not have permission from their people to do so. Seeing as the Indians didn't recognize the legitimacy or the authority of these representatives, the treaty was invalid.

This portrait of Arthur St. Clair, painted by Charles Willson Peale, was based on a miniature portrait Peale had painted after St. Clair had commissioned him. St. Clair kept his position as governor of the Northwest Territory until U.S. president Thomas Jefferson removed him from office because St. Clair was against the statehood of Ohio in 1802.

⇌ Another Attempt ⇌

The Treaty of Fort McIntosh increased the tensions between Indians and the government of the United States. Adding to the explosive situation was the increased threat from the Iroquois Confederacy. Many officials worried that the nations that had supported the British during the American Revolution would now join forces with the tribes of the Ohio Valley to fight for their homelands. Shortly after the Treaty of Fort McIntosh was signed, the Northwest Territory erupted in violence as American settlers moved onto land that the Native Americans claimed. Without the funds to deal with the problem militarily, the United States government sought a peaceful diplomatic solution. Secretary of War Henry Knox urged Arthur St. Clair (the governor of the Northwest Territory) to restore order as quickly as possible and to establish peaceful relations between the settlers and the Indians. Knox instructed St. Clair to spare no effort in settling the land disputes with the Six Nations and the Ohio Valley tribes.

A black and white landscape drawing depicts pentagon-shaped Fort Harmar, the meeting place of Arthur St. Clair and the Indian chiefs. The fort, which was built in 1785 by General Josiah Harmar and his troops, was surrounded by a tall wooden fence in order to protect the area from invading enemies.

Early in December 1788, St. Clair called a meeting with the Indian chiefs at Fort Harmar. It was attended by representatives of the Wyandot, Delaware, Ottawa, Chippewa, Potawatomi, and Sauk tribes. Tribal leaders asked St. Clair to establish an Indian reservation on the land west of the Muskingum River and north of the Ohio River. However, St. Clair refused. Instead, he demanded that the chiefs honor existing agreements, observe the reservations created in the Treaty of Fort McIntosh, and abide by the boundaries established in the Treaty of Fort Stanwix. If the Indians refused, St. Clair would threaten war. Reluctantly, on January 9, 1789, the chiefs signed the Treaty of Fort Harmar, which reinforced the provisions of previous treaties.

This meant that, once again, the Indian tribes found themselves leaving the negotiating table with less than they had come with. In effect, government representatives had once again dismissed or ignored Indian land claims and bullied the Indians into submission. After the Treaty of Fort Harmar, a number of tribal leaders became convinced that the Americans would not stop until they had all the western lands. In response, some tribes refused to honor the agreement and increased attacks on white settlers in the Northwest Territory. As the level of violence rose, American officials were at last forced to admit that their Indian policy was a failure. Growing fears of an all-out frontier war heightened when it seemed that the nations of the Iroquois Confederacy would enter the fight.

3

A New Indian Policy

y the summer of 1789, many government officials were dismayed by the deteriorating relations with the Indians. Henry Knox, the secretary of war, was anxious to prevent an outbreak of violence between white Americans and the Indians. Because of this desire, he sought changes in the government's policy toward Indian groups. Based on the Indians' earlier responses to the treaty talks, the government's manner of working with Indian groups had clearly failed.

⁓ Seeking a Solution ⁓

In a letter written to President George Washington in June 1789, Knox outlined a new Native American policy. First, in an attempt to settle the growing disturbances in the west, Knox suggested that there were two ways to deal with the problem. The first was to raise an army that would primarily be used to deal with warring tribes. The second was to continue to make treaties with the Indians. In these treaties, their rights and land boundaries would be clearly defined. Knox also wanted to be sure that the government would

Part of Knox's letter to Washington reads: "In examining the question how the disturbances on the frontiers are to be quieted, two modes present themselves, by which the object might perhaps be effected; the first of which is by raising an army, and [destroying the resisting] tribes entirely, or . . ." See page 57 for a partial transcription of the letter.

punish those whites who violated any of the provisions of the treaty.

Nonetheless, each solution presented its own set of problems. Trying to put together an army was a costly affair. There was also the question of whether or not the United States had the right to use an army to deal with the Indian "problem." As Knox stated to President Washington, which was quoted in the article titled "On the Road to Canandaigua," "It is presumable [can be taken for granted] that a nation solicitous of [concerned with] establishing its character on the broad basis of justice, would not only hesitate at, but reject every proposition [plan] to benefit itself, by the injury of any neighboring community." Knox also emphasized that in principle, the Indian tribes had a right to their lands. He also believed that the interests of the United States would

Henry Knox is pictured here in an oil-on-canvas portrait by Charles Willson Peale, circa 1784. Knox, who was born in Boston on July 25, 1750, became an adviser to General George Washington at the start of the American Revolution. The first secretary of war in the United States, Knox also was instrumental in commissioning the first ships for the U.S. Navy.

be better served if the federal government recognized this fact in its future dealings with Indian tribes. Knox's thoughts on this matter provided the basis for the newly emerging Indian policy that would follow in the years to come.

⮞ Rising Concerns ⮜

Knox had other reasons to be concerned about the current state of affairs between the United States and various Native American groups. A number of troubling issues had come up since the end of the Revolutionary War and the Treaty of Paris. If these issues were not resolved soon, the consequences for the new nation could be disastrous.

One of the most pressing problems was that of land. The government was already plagued by boundary disputes between white settlers and the Indians, particularly in the Ohio Valley territory. Land speculators selling fraudulent land claims to whites in Indian territory were a growing headache. And, increasingly, whites were venturing onto land that had been set aside for Indians. As a result, murder and violence were on the rise.

The growing fear of war threatened the very existence of the United States. Another war would be too costly, both in terms of money and manpower. In addition, the Loyalists who had fled to Canada during the Revolutionary War hoped to regain the former territory held by Great Britain in the Northwest. If they were successful, they would create an Indian buffer state. This would protect Canada from the United States and any attempt by the American government to try to take Canadian land once again. Moreover, fear of British intervention was reason enough to work out a better policy of dealing with the Indians.

Perhaps most troubling of all was the growing threat of the Six Nations, whose political and military power was still very strong. Knox feared that if tensions in the Ohio Valley continued to rise, the Six Nations might decide to give their support to the Ohio tribes. Such a move would surely signal the beginning of a long and bloody war.

⚊ A Course of Action ⚊

In September 1790, Secretary Knox reluctantly began making plans for a military operation on the Wabash River. The area had been the scene of much violence between Indians and whites. Knox hoped that through a show of military force, he would be able to subdue the Indian tribes without having to go to war. He had not given up hope that the problem could be solved through diplomatic channels. President George Washington was in full support of this action. Washington realized that in order for the federal government to have any hope of succeeding with the Six

This is a miniature portrait of George Washington by Benjamin Trott. This image of Washington was painted on ivory, which comes from the tusks (and, sometimes, large teeth) of elephants, walruses, and whales. As opposed to paper, canvas, or vellum, ivory became popular for miniatures in the eighteenth and nineteenth centuries.

Nations, it was important to make sure that the man chosen as the government's representative would be honest and fair when it came to resolving differences with the Indians.

Washington's choice of Timothy Pickering for the position was a good one. Pickering, a Harvard graduate and veteran of the Revolutionary War, had been picked by the new government to be its first postmaster general. Upon meeting Pickering on a street in Philadelphia, Washington had been impressed with Pickering's intellect and attitude. Because of this chance meeting, Washington asked him if he would take on the duties of the Indian commissioner. Realizing the importance of what was being asked of him, Pickering agreed. He was determined, as Washington is quoted as saying in John C. Mohawk's article "The Canandaigua Treaty of 1794 in Historical Perspective," to "take the hatchet out of the heads of the Six Nations and bury it."

Meeting at Tioga

In October 1790, Pickering traveled to Tioga Point, located 80 miles (129 kilometers) north of Wilkes-Barre, Pennsylvania.

Here, he was to meet with the members of the Seneca tribe to discuss the growing problems between the Six Nations and the American government. In mid-November, the Seneca delegation arrived and the talks began in earnest.

One of the key complaints the Senecas voiced to Pickering was over a legal matter. Earlier that summer, white settlers had murdered two Seneca Indians who had been hunting for food. The incident had heightened tensions in northern Pennsylvania, and the Indians were not satisfied with the government's efforts to bring the murderers to justice. At the very least, the Indians wanted blood revenge. This meant that they would bring the murderers to justice themselves or they would arrive at some kind of compensation to make sure that those who were responsible for the two deaths were punished in some manner.

Pickering soon learned that in dealing with the Indians, he needed to be familiar with their customs and the manner in which they dealt with discussing important issues. For instance, he realized that gifts of food, drink, and wampum were very important; these offerings were seen as a measure of respect and friendship among the different tribes. Pickering paid close attention as the Indian leaders explained the nature of their culture. Despite Pickering's ignorance in treaty matters, the conference went smoothly. As he later reported, as quoted in Jack Campisi and William Starna's article, "On the Road to Canandaigua: The Treaty of 1794," part of the ease came with the fact that "there were no lands to be bargained for, no boundaries to be disputed, and no alliances to be formed." However, what Pickering had actually succeeded in doing was renewing the offers of friendship with the Senecas and making sure that the government took their concerns seriously.

⸺ A Heartfelt Plea ⸺

Shortly after the Tioga Conference ended in December 1790, President Washington received a passionate plea from three leaders of the Seneca nation: Cornplanter, Half-Town, and Big Tree. The men had traveled to Philadelphia with Pickering and a delegation of other Seneca chiefs. In a powerful address delivered to the president, Cornplanter reminded Washington of his promise to "secure us the possession of our lands," and the Senecas' disappointment at the outcome of the Fort Stanwix Treaty in 1784, which forced the Senecas to give up most of their land.

According to "On the Road to Canandaigua," the chiefs admitted, "We have already said how we came to join against you; we saw that we were wrong; we wished for peace; and you demanded that a great country be given up to you." The Senecas willingly gave up the land as the price for peace. However, in doing so, they asked that they be allowed to hold on to what "little land which you have left for us." The chiefs also stated, as documented in the same article, that:

> All the lands we have been speaking of belong to the Six Nations, no part of it ever belonged to the King of England and he could not give it to you. The land we live on our fathers received from God, and they transmitted it to us for our children, and we cannot part with it.

This lithograph (a print made from a drawing on a slab of stone) of Cornplanter is based on an oil portrait of him that was executed in 1796 in New York City. Cornplanter, whose English name was John O'Bail (named for his Dutch father), had the difficult job of peacekeeper for the Senecas. Ultimately, he was given a tract of land for his help.

Hence, it did not matter to the Senecas whether the issue was the western lands of the Ohio territory that belonged to the Six Nations or the Iroquois land that was given to the Senecas. From their standpoint, the United States government had no right to take away land whether it be through a treaty or as the result of surrender.

⚊ Washington's Response ⚊

Washington wasted little time in replying to the letter from the Seneca leaders. He reported to the chiefs that a newly appointed Indian commissioner (Timothy Pickering) would be looking into the complaints of the Six Nations more closely. Washington sincerely wanted to end the threat of Indian hostilities while seeking more peaceful relations with the Six Nations tribes. He promised the chiefs that only the federal government had the power to make treaties with Native American nations, particularly in terms of sales of land.

Furthermore, as Washington stated, any treaty made without the consent of the government was not binding. Indians had the right to pursue their complaints in a court of law. Last and perhaps most important, Washington promised that only the Indians had the right to sell their lands or to refuse to sell them. These important ideas would eventually (in one form or another) find their way into the Canandaigua Treaty in 1794.

In addition, Washington asked the Senecas to work harder at assimilating some of the white man's ways. For example, he suggested that they take up farming. Washington pledged to help the Senecas in the hopes that other Six Nation tribes would do the same. In addition, Washington promised to work harder at bringing to trial whites who had been accused of killing Indians. Washington realized that gaining the trust and loyalty of the Indians was crucial to the federal government's ability to handle the trouble in the Ohio territory. It was also clear that keeping the Iroquois from joining forces with the western tribes was crucial if the United States hoped to avoid war.

4

Walking the Road to Peace

n April 1791, the United States government tried to interest the Six Nations in a conference in the hope of persuading them not to join in the escalating hostilities in the Ohio Valley. Washington also wanted to recruit Native American warriors for the American army. He realized that time was running out: violence against members of the Six Nations had increased. Many Iroquois Indians were being murdered by whites, and meanwhile, the government remained powerless to stop whites from harming the Indians. In addition, pressure from the white community, which was demanding more frontier land, and the mounting anger of the Seneca tribe over the Fort Stanwix Treaty had put the administration in a difficult position.

⚊ Another Meeting ⚊

Growing more concerned over the situation, Secretary of War Knox asked Pickering to meet with the Six Nations once again. Pickering was to tell the tribes that their well-being depended on the protection and friendship of the United States. He sent a message to the chiefs and other tribal

This oil-on-canvas painting by Henry Cheever Pratt shows the Ohio River in 1855. An idyllic slice of the American landscape, this was part of the Ohio Valley territory that was being disputed by the Senecas and the Americans. The Senecas in this region were related to the Senecas in New York.

leaders of the Six Nations. In the message, he asked that they attend a council meeting in June of 1791. He also reminded the Indians of his own conduct as being (according to the article "On the Road to Canandaigua: The Treaty of 1794") "open and sincere" in his determination to help the tribes.

It was decided that the meeting would be held at Newtown Point in western New York where Pickering managed the transport of the many provisions and gifts that he would offer to the Indians upon their arrival. Finally, on July 2, everyone was assembled and the talks began.

However, even before the talks commenced, Pickering learned that many of the Iroquois who were attending were very suspicious of the American government's motives. Despite their misgivings, they reassured Pickering that they wished to remain on good terms with the United States. According to the book *Treaty of Canandaigua 1794*, they also wished to help bring about a peace with their "Brothers of the Western Nations . . . and endeavour to bring them to an accommodation with the people of the thirteen States." Above all, they wanted to stop the bloodshed. Nonetheless, Pickering would not rest until he had formal assurances from the tribes that they would remain neutral.

Pickering spoke first. He told the Indian leaders that he was there in friendship and that the issue of the western tribes and war needed to be resolved. He also spoke to them about their fears concerning their land. As quoted in the article "On the Road to Canandaigua," Pickering stated: "I can think but of two grounds of the jealousy which you may entertain of your brothers of the United States. One lest, they should attempt to take your lands from you; and the other, lest in order to get your lands, and in revenge for injuries, they should attempt to destroy you or drive you away."

⌐ Another Successful Meeting ⌐

Pickering also addressed the council over the issues of land. He reminded them of the Indian Trade and Intercourse Act of 1790. This act regulated the sale of Indian land and oversaw trade activities with Native American groups. Pickering emphasized that the act, which made selling and trading with Indians illegal without a license, was for the protection of Indian tribes. The act was fully supported by President Washington, who, Pickering stated, would continue to help protect the Six Nations and their lands.

Seneca leader Red Jacket is featured in this stone lithograph dating from circa 1835. Red Jacket, whose Indian name was Sagoyewatha, lived from approximately 1750 to 1830. During his lifetime, Red Jacket experienced the American Revolution and the War of 1812. Red Jacket grew up on Seneca lands in upstate New York.

While the Indian leaders respected Washington and his words, they also told Pickering that they would nonetheless remain on guard. As Seneca leader Red Jacket explained to Pickering (documented in the book *Treaty of Canandaigua 1794*), "We wish Congress to be very careful how they speak; and to speak nothing of us but peace; and we desire they would do the same among their own people." But for the time being, the Six Nations seemed willing to remain neutral in the matter of the western tribes and the troubles in the Ohio territory. Tribal leaders also promised to send their own peacekeepers to the western Indians in the hope of working out a peaceful resolution among them.

For Pickering, the meeting at Newtown was a success. He was able to explain to the Six Nations what the federal government's policy would be in the West. As well, they reassured the tribes of the American government's pledge of friendship and its promise to protect Indian lands. He listened to the grievances of the tribes firsthand. Even though Pickering failed in enlisting any Indians into the American military, he secured their promise not to join forces with the western tribes.

⇌ A Turn for the Worse ⇌

However, only three months later, disaster struck. Even as Pickering was meeting with the Six Nations tribes, the American government had dispatched troops to stop the rising tide of attacks by the western tribes. In October 1791, under the leadership of General Arthur St. Clair, American troops were defeated by a group of Miami warriors. It was a decisive victory for the western tribes and a humiliating defeat for the Americans. Thrilled with their success, the western tribes encouraged the leaders of the Six Nations to join them in their fight against the Americans.

Secretary Knox also wanted to enlist the help of the Six Nations. He proposed that instead of having them act as peacekeepers, the Six Nations side with the Americans in their fight with the western Indians. Upon learning of Knox's plan, Pickering was furious. In the end, Knox backed down from the proposal.

⇌ Gathering Clouds ⇌

For the remaining months of 1792, there was very little change in the situation in the Ohio Valley. In the meantime, the United States took a two-prong approach to the problem. Even as the government prepared to go to war, representatives

This woodcut shows canoes on the Ohio River in what was called Ohio Country, the name given to the territory consisting of modern-day Ohio, eastern Indiana, western Pennsylvania, and northwestern West Virginia. Ohio Country Indians were largely self-sufficient. They made what they needed from materials that were available in their environment, such as these birch bark canoes.

were working to establish peaceful relations with the western tribes.

The Indians did the same. In August 1793, another meeting was held, this time near the Wabash River. Tribal leaders representing both the western and Iroquois tribes came together to try to create a unified response to the American peace proposal. By November, the tribes had reached an agreement, which they forwarded to Washington. The request was simple: the Indians wanted their lands north of the Ohio River returned to them.

⸺ Meeting at Sandusky ⸺

In July 1793, Pickering, accompanied by two other commissioners, set out for Sandusky in the Ohio territory. However, when they arrived at the mouth of the Niagara River, British agents refused to give them permission to travel any farther. Instead, the three men were forced to speak to tribal messengers, who repeated the Indians' demand that the United States return the lands north of the Ohio.

Pickering tried to reach some kind of agreement with the messengers. He told them that the United States was willing to make amends with regard to the Fort Harmar Treaty, and agreed that the government had made a mistake in declaring it had complete rights to the territory east of the Mississippi River. Pickering also told the Indians that the government was willing to offer compensation for lands that had been lost to them. However, he could not agree to the Indians' demand for the return of the Ohio lands. Americans were already settled in the territory, and it would be too difficult to make them move. The messengers carried Pickering's response to tribal leaders.

On August 16, Pickering received the Indians' decision. As described in *Treaty of Canandaigua 1794*, Pickering was told:

> We desire you to consider Brothers, that our only demand is the peaceable possession of a small part of our once great Country—Look back and view the lands from whence we have been driven, to this spot:—We can retreat no further because the Country behind, hardly affords food for its present inhabitants; and we have therefore resolved to leave our bones, in this, small space, to which we are now confin'd.

The message was clear: the western tribes were ready to go to war. The United States had little choice; there was no way to avoid a war.

⇌ Buffalo Creek ⇌

On October 8, 1793, a council was held at an Onondaga village at Buffalo Creek (located between New York and Pennsylvania). All the Iroquois nations, except the Mohawks, and several western tribes gathered there. Also in attendance were John Butler, a representative for the British, and Israel Chapin, the superintendent of Indian affairs for the United States. Once again, the western tribes appealed to the Iroquois to join them in their fight against the Americans. Although concerned, the Iroquois refused to commit themselves to any particular plan.

In fact, the Iroquois were drawing up their own proposal to be presented to the Americans. Their most important demand concerned land: they asked that their rights to the lands they had held along the Ohio River be reinstated. The exception would be those areas where whites had already settled. The Iroquois also made clear to Chapin that they would be very disappointed if the government did not honor their request.

In February 1794, the government responded to the Iroquois proposal. However, rather than give a direct answer, the Americans asked that another council be held where they could continue their discussions with the Indians. The Iroquois were dismayed by the response. In reply to government officials, Iroquois leaders said (as stated in the article "On the Road to Canandaigua"):

> The speech you have brought us, has given us great uneasiness, we are greatly at loss how to act we expected a direct answer to our proposals of a boundary line; now we are much distressed that you gave us half an answer.

Once again, the Iroquois voiced their demands to the American government: unless their request for a boundary was agreed upon, the Iroquois would not work with the western tribes. The Iroquois also refused to attend the proposed council. It appeared that a standoff had been reached.

5

The Growing Threat of War

y 1794, things were looking bleak. There seemed little hope of a council meeting between the United States government and the various Indian nations. Native American leaders were becoming increasingly dissatisfied over the recent turn of events. The government was also worried about the growing number of white settlers in Pennsylvania who were moving onto lands known as the Erie Triangle and Presqu'Isle, both of which had been taken from the Seneca tribe. Hostilities between whites and Indians continued to rise, as did the complaints by the western tribes and the Six Nations over the treaties that had taken their lands away.

⚊ Another Attempt at Peace ⚊

In mid-June, Israel Chapin once again traveled to meet with leaders of the Six Nations at Buffalo Creek. By this time, he had learned that the Iroquois leaders had complained to Pennsylvania state officials about the presence of troops and land surveyors in the Presqu'Isle area. The situation was becoming more serious by the minute.

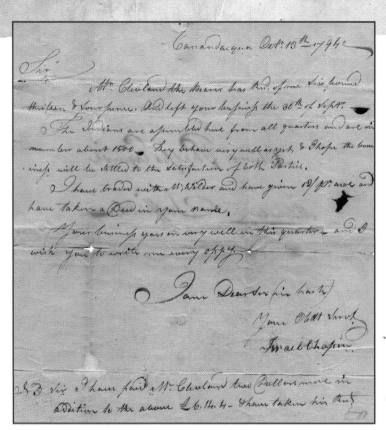

At left is part of a brief letter written by General Israel Chapin in Canandaigua, New York, to Oliver Phelps, Esquire, in Suffield, Connecticut, on October 13, 1794. The letter was written less than a month prior to the signing of the Treaty of Canandaigua. Chapin was an explorer, a land developer, and an agent for the Indians in this region. For a transcription of the letter, see page 57.

On June 18, 1794, the council formally began. Along with the leaders and warriors of the Six Nations, Chapin and two interpreters were present. Almost immediately, Iroquois leaders pressed Chapin on the issue of land. They made it very clear that they formally rejected the Fort Stanwix and McIntosh treaties. Speaking for the group, the Seneca leader Cornplanter told Chapin that the Indians no longer trusted Congress because Congress had repeatedly betrayed the Iroquois and other tribes. Cornplanter also told Chapin that the Iroquois were ready to let their warriors speak for them. As quoted in *Treaty of Canandaigua 1794*, he told Chapin, "We now call upon you for an answer, as Congress and their commissioners have oftentimes deceived us and, if these difficulties are not removed, the consequences will be bad." Chapin realized that Cornplanter was not making an idle threat. Clearly, the

Iroquois were ready to go to war if the Senecas' land was not restored to them. The government needed to act quickly if it wanted to avoid a full-blown conflict with the Indians.

⚊ Buying Time ⚊

Even as Chapin was meeting with the Iroquois leaders, the United States government was taking steps to ease tensions. On the orders of President Washington, the governor of Pennsylvania stopped surveying at Presqu'Isle and halted construction of a military outpost in the area. However, the governor also asked that Washington resolve the land issue with the tribes as soon as possible. At the same time, he told the president that as governor, he would not surrender the land in question to the Indians.

In the meantime, Chapin continued talks with representatives of the Six Nations. In letters sent to Secretary Knox, he outlined the objections of the tribes. Besides the problem of surveyors in the Presqu'Isle region, the Indians were also opposed to building a military fort. Chapin asked that the government work harder at negotiating a settlement with the tribes. Knox passed on Chapin's recommendations to both President Washington and the governor of Pennsylvania.

It was Washington who then directed Chapin to set up another council meeting with the Six Nations—this time at Canandaigua, located in western New York. If all went well, the meeting scheduled for September 1794 would settle the outstanding problems between the government and the Indians. Washington also asked that Timothy Pickering negotiate for the government. Chapin was then ordered to deliver the invitations to the proposed meeting to the leaders of the Six Nations. All except one chief accepted the invitation.

⚊ A Meeting in New York ⚊

On September 19, Pickering arrived at Canandaigua, where he found a message waiting for him: the Iroquois chiefs had changed their minds about meeting at Canandaigua and instead asked that it be moved to Buffalo Creek. They wanted time to gather their fall harvest, and they wished to avoid the strain of traveling to Canandaigua. Pickering realized that if he agreed to the demand, he would not only be meeting with the Indians, but also with British agents—something he refused to do. He would not comply with the request, stating that he did not have the proper authority to move the meeting. The meeting would either be held at the stated location or not at all.

While waiting for the Indians to arrive, Pickering made preparations for food and gifts for his guests. It was estimated that close to 1,000 members of the Iroquois nation would be in attendance. In addition to the necessities, Pickering also commissioned an Indian to make a large wampum belt, which cost him two dollars, the equivalent of about thirty-three American dollars today. A delegation of Quakers helped Pickering get ready for the meeting. The Indians trusted the Quakers as well as Israel Chapin.

In late September, the first of the Iroquois nations arrived with the Oneida delegation, numbering around 135 people. By mid-October, the remaining tribes had arrived. Altogether, more than 1,500 Indians had come to Canandaigua. Many of the tribes were dressed in their finest clothing and decorated with bright paint. As documented in *Treaty of Canandaigua 1794*, one observer recorded the grand entrance made by the leaders of the Iroquois:

> The Oneidas, Caugas, and Onondagoes were drawn up, dressed and painted with their arms prepared for a salute before General Chapin's Door. The Men able to bear arms, marched in, assuming a good Deal of importance and drew up in a line facing the Oneidas &c., Colonel Pickering, General Chapin, and many white people present. The Indians fired three rounds, which the other Indians answered by a like number, making a long and loud Echo through the Woods. Their commanders then ordered them to form a circle around the commissioner and General Chapin; then sitting down on the ground, they delivered a speech.

⇐ Getting Down to Business ⇒

The first few days of the meeting were spent on treaty protocol, or a plan deciding how the treaty talks should progress. This included formal expressions of condolences for those people who had died since the tribes had last met. Pickering also performed a symbolic ceremony of burying a Delaware Indian who had been murdered by an American. In closing, Pickering spoke to the leaders, reminding them that the United States would keep open the path of peace "as long as the sun shone," according to the book *The Great Law and Longhouse: A Political History of the Iroquois Confederacy*. For many of the Indians, Pickering's phrase would come to hold a special and treasured meaning. In the meantime, Pickering also met privately with several Indian leaders.

On October 27, Pickering received important news. Some months earlier, on August 20, 1794, American general Anthony Wayne had led American forces against a number of western alliance tribes. When faced with a large military force, the Indians failed to mount an effective resistance. Wayne defeated them and in effect crushed the western alliance. While both the Iroquois and the Americans had earlier received news of the battle, accounts had been so sketchy that both sides claimed victory. Pickering then learned that in fact, the Americans had won a decisive victory. With the western tribes neutralized, the Iroquois Confederacy was alone. Pickering clearly had the upper hand, but still needed to move with caution so as not to anger the Indians and drive them away.

⸺ Coming to Terms ⸺

For the Indians attending the council, there were three main issues to be discussed: the murders of Indians by white settlers, which were going unpunished; the dispute over the land issues under the Fort Stanwix Treaty; and the settlement of Presqu'Isle. For the Senecas, the provisions of the Fort Stanwix Treaty were illegal because the chiefs who had negotiated the treaty failed to submit it to the Grand Council (the Senecas' highest governing authority) for ratification.

The negotiations continued and seemed to be making progress until November 9, when Cornplanter (one of the council's more important leaders) complained to Pickering

> By His Excellency ANTHONY WAYNE, Esquire, Major General & Commander in Chief of the Legion, and Commissioner Plenipotentiary, of the United States of America, for establishing a permanent peace with all the Indian tribes and nations, North-west of the Ohio.
>
> L. S. *A PROCLAMATION.*
>
> WHEREAS, I the said Plenipotentiary, in virtue of the power and authority in me vested, have entered into certain preliminary articles with the following tribes and nations of Indians viz. The Wyandots, Chepawas, Ottawas, Putawatimies, Miamis, Shawanoes and Delawares, for a cessa-

The Proclamation of General Anthony Wayne, part of which is seen above, was issued six months after the Battle of Fallen Timbers. Wayne was instrumental in training the Legion of the United States, which ultimately defeated the Indians during the battle. This document announces the beginning of a peace process with many Indian tribes.

---

of the United States government's past treatment of the Indians. He then stated that if a treaty were signed, it would be signed only by the leaders and not by the warriors who had also come to the council. Cornplanter also threatened to leave the treaty proceedings because of complaints by some of the other Indians over what they saw as a high-handed treatment of the other leaders. Pickering moved quickly to keep Cornplanter at Canandaigua. He understood that it was important to have him at the treaty signing. However, he did not agree to Cornplanter's suggestion, as he realized that it was important for all who attended to sign the final treaty.

⚊ "The Two Rusty Places" ⚊

At the same time that Pickering was listening to the concerns of the Indians, he was also doing his best to indicate that the United States government took the complaints made by the Iroquois seriously. Speaking before the Six Nations members, Pickering told the group, as described in "On the Road to Canandaigua: The Treaty of 1794," that he would now remove "the two rusty places" that centered on the land disputes from the "Chain of Friendship" between the Six Nations and the federal government.

Then, Pickering proposed to return the land along Lake Erie (where the Six Nations had settlements) to the Senecas. He also offered the tribes hunting rights on the lands given to the United States through the Fort Stanwix Treaty, as well as all other lands given by the Iroquois to the United States. In addition, he promised that all settlements of the Six Nations would be undisturbed. In an attempt to reach some kind of agreement, Pickering suggested that the Senecas give up a strip of land 4 miles (about 6.5 km) wide along the south bank of the Niagara River. Finally, Pickering offered the tribes an annual payment by the United States government of $4,500, or approximately $75,000 in today's American dollars.

After two days of conferring, the tribal leaders came to Pickering with their answer: nothing would be done until the United States withdrew its claim on the strip of land along the Niagara River. The Senecas stated the proposed piece of land would threaten their fishing and settlement. Pickering then told them that the government would pay for the land. Nonetheless, his proposal was turned down. Realizing that the land in question was the one remaining obstacle to completing a treaty, Pickering relented. He asked that a road (to be owned by the Senecas) be built that would run to a nearby fort. If the Indians agreed, Pickering would not push the land claim any further.

⇒ One Last Problem ⇒

By November 9, two large pieces of parchment were waiting for the signatures of the council's participants. According to the book *Great Law and Longhouse: A Political History of the Iroquois Confederacy*, one of the Quaker observers wrote, "We were in hopes the business would now close, but to our surprise and disappointment, we soon discovered some dissatisfaction among the Indians." It turned out that the warriors would not sign the treaty. Speaking for the group, Cornplanter told Pickering that the Six Nations had been deceived by the government officials with the Fort Stanwix Treaty over land cessions. Pickering patiently explained that these complaints were old and that he had also disapproved of that treaty.

Regardless, Pickering was not willing to risk failure. When questioned as to why the Indians were unwilling to include specific references to lands ceded in the Fort Stanwix and McIntosh treaties, Pickering did not receive an answer. When Pickering asked if this meant the Indians would formally agree that they no longer had any claims over the land cessions, he still received no answer. When he again asked for an explanation, according to the *Treaty of Canandaigua 1794*, one Indian leader finally told him, "They [the chiefs] are afraid of offending the British."

6

The Treaty of Canandaigua

O n November 11, 1794, the two sides met at last to sign the treaty. According to *Treaty of Canandaigua 1794*, one of the Quakers present recorded, first, "the Eel, an Onondaga chief spoke to the Indians . . . Colonel Pickering held up the two parchments containing the articles of the treaty and asked if we should proceed." Later that afternoon, fifty-nine of the Six Nations chiefs signed the Treaty of Canandaigua. More than two months in the making, the treaty signaled a new chapter for the United States government and the Six Nations. As Pickering later wrote to Secretary of War Knox shortly after the treaty's signing, "I have pleasure to inform you that yesterday Peace and Friendship with the Six Nations was established."

⸗ The Treaty Terms ⸗

The text of the treaty was in fact quite simple. It consisted of seven articles outlining the terms to which Pickering and the Six Nations Indians had finally agreed. The treaty's primary focus was on the issues that most troubled the Six Nations, particularly the Senecas. As for the United States, its main objective was to settle the question of land claims by the Six Nations and to create a policy of negotiations and payment for land bought from the Six Nations.

Article I of the treaty proclaims, "Peace and Friendship are hereby firmly established, and shall be perpetual, between the United States and the Six Nations." This is an important element of the treaty. It marks the hopeful direction that the United States government sought to take in creating policy with the Six Nations and other Native American groups.

Articles II, III, and IV of the treaty deal specifically with the land issues. In Article II, the federal government guaranteed the Oneida, Onondaga, and Cayuga nations clear ownership of their lands. Furthermore, the article stated that at no time would the United States government claim these lands or in any way disturb those who inhabited them. Article III defined the boundaries of the Senecas' lands, while at the same time carefully omitting the claims that the Six Nations might have had to lands in the Ohio region. This article also recognized Seneca ownership of the strip along the Niagara River for which Pickering had so unsuccessfully negotiated. Article IV of the treaty reinforced the promise of the Six Nations never to claim lands outside of the boundaries specified in the treaty.

Article V of the treaty outlined the compromise reached by Pickering and the Six Nations over the area near the Niagara River. This provision allowed the United States the right to use a road that was owned by the Senecas along the Niagara River, giving it access to the waterways. This was crucial for settlement because it gave farmers and other settlers in the Kentucky-Ohio region a way to transport their goods to market.

Article VI of the treaty outlined the financial compensation by the United States government to the Six Nations. Under the terms of the treaty, the United States promised to pay $10,000 in goods, including tools, cloth, and other items, along with a yearly payment of $4,500 to the tribes. This was a considerable sum for the time and it symbolized the deep commitment of the Americans to deal fairly with the Indians.

Justice for crimes committed against Indians was the focus of Article VII of the treaty. Under the agreement, both sides promised not to take any private or unofficial act of revenge when a serious crime such as robbery, murder, or assault was committed against either the Americans or the Indians. Instead, each group would submit a written complaint to the other and the appropriate action would be taken to punish those who were found guilty of such crimes.

⸺ The Treaty's Importance ⸺

The Canandaigua Treaty was an important diplomatic document for both the United States and the Six Nations. The treaty provided the United States with a measure of security at a time when tensions with Great Britain and other Native American groups could have forced the nation into a costly war. The treaty also marked the beginning of a policy toward Native Americans that the United States adopted in order to ensure its own survival. By working hard to maintain good relations with the Six Nations, the government had taken the necessary steps to protect the interests of the still new nation.

This oil-on-canvas portrait of George Washington was painted by Joseph Wright of Derby, an English artist. Wright depicts Washington as rather rotund. According to the book, George Washington's Mount Vernon: At Home in Revolutionary America, *from July 21–22, 1775, Washington bought a pig, an unknown number of ducks, "1 dozen pigeons, veal, 1 dozen squash, 2 dozen eggs, hurtle-berries, biscuits and a cork cask."*

In addition, the treaty secured the United States' claim to the Ohio Valley. This strengthened the claim for the land by the United States against those of other nations, particularly Great Britain. The treaty also returned the land given up by the Senecas under the Fort Stanwix Treaty and secured the land claims held by the Six Nations. Above all, the treaty recognized the Six Nations as a sovereign, or self-governing, confederacy dealing with another nation, the United States.

⸗ A Hopeful Beginning? ⸗

President Washington formally signed the treaty into law on January 21, 1795. It is still a recognized agreement between the Iroquois Nations and the United States government. For Timothy Pickering, the treaty was a step toward improved

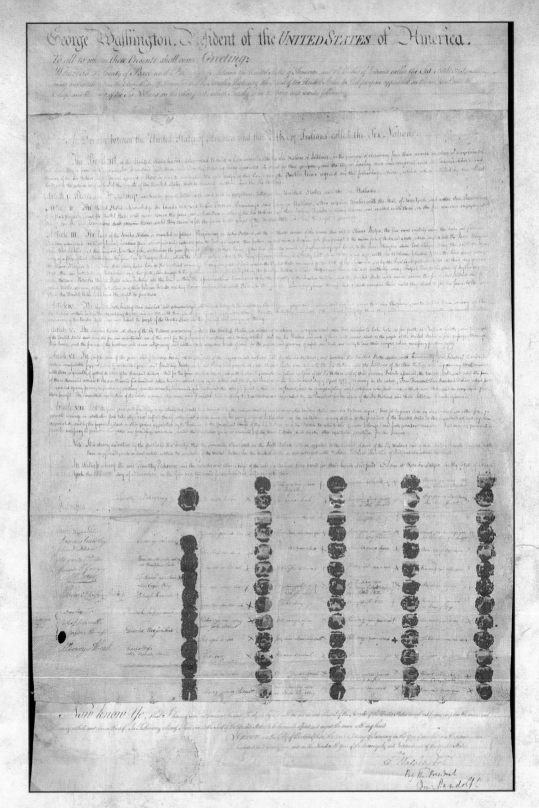

This copy of the *Treaty of Canandaigua*, housed in the National Archives in Washington, D.C., is one of two existing copies of the treaty. It shows the wax seals that were used to authenticate the signatures of all of those who signed this monumentally important document.

relations between the two nations. In a letter written one week after the meeting at Canandaigua, as documented in *Treaty of Canandaigua 1794*, Pickering wrote:

> I did not come here [Canandaigua] to drive a bargain; but to manifest the real desires of the United States to live in friendship with the Six Nations. I therefore did not consider how much I could gain for the United States; but as far as circumstances would permit, how I should promote the true interests of the Six Nations. In thus consulting their interests, I expected to give them satisfaction: and I am not disappointed.

In light of those developments, Pickering had every reason to be optimistic. However, as history would reveal, in many of its dealings with Native Americans the United States fell short. Against what were often tragic and dishonorable actions on the part of the United States, the Treaty of Canandaigua is that much more remarkable for its honesty, integrity, and sincere wish to establish cordial relations with the Indian nations.

Timeline

October 1783 Committee on Indian Affairs of the Continental Congress issues report for settlement of the West; suggests that boundary line between the states and Indian land be established.

1784 Treaty of Fort Stanwix signed; Seneca Nation forced to give up most of its land; Six Nations tribes are recognized by the United States as conquered peoples.

1785 Treaty of Fort McIntosh signed; western Indians surrender most of their land in the Northwest; United States does not recognize the Iroquois Confederacy.

1789 Ohio tribes reject treaty and begin attacks on settlers.

1791 Timothy Pickering, postmaster general of the United States, is appointed by President Washington to negotiate a peace with the Six Nations.

1792 Secretary of War Knox asks for a meeting in Philadelphia with leaders of the Iroquois Nation, in the hope that he can persuade them not to join forces with the western tribes and instead ally themselves with the United States.

Summer Iroquois and western tribes meet in order to present
≈ **1792** a united front to the United States, which is preparing
to go to war if a peace is not reached.

October 8, Council held at Onondaga Village at Buffalo Creek
≈ **1793** located between New York and Pennsylvania; British
and American representatives attend. Western tribes
ask the Six Nations to ally with them against the
United States government.

≈ **1794** Another meeting is proposed between the United
States and the Six Nations at Buffalo Creek to try to
reach some sort of agreement over land. Indian
representatives make clear that unless their
demands are met, war is inevitable.

Summer President Washington agrees to another treaty talk,
≈ **1794** this time at Canandaigua, New York, in September.

September 19, Pickering arrives at Canandaigua. Over the course
≈ **1794** of the next few weeks, representatives from the Six
Nations arrive to participate.

November 11, Treaty of Canandaigua signed by Pickering as a
≈ **1794** representative of the United States and fifty-nine
sachems representing the Six Nations. The treaty
recognizes the sovereignty of the Six Nations,
returns land to the Senecas, and secures land for the
United States in the Ohio Valley.

≈ **1994** 200th anniversary of the Canandaigua Treaty
celebrated; it is the longest recognized treaty
between the United States and an Indian nation.

Whereas a Treaty of Peace and Fri...
made and concl... on the Eleventh day of Nove...
Chiefs and War... of the Six Nations on the...

Primary Source Transcriptions

Page 15: Excerpt from the Treaty of Fort Stanwix

Transcription

Articles concluded at Fort Stanwix, on the twenty-second day of October, one thousand seven hundred and eighty-four, between Oliver Wolcott, Richard Butler, and Arthur Lee, Commissioners Plenipotentiary from the United States, in Congress assembled, on the one Part, and the Sachems and Warriors of the Six Nations, on the other.

The United States of America give peace to the Senecas, Mohawks, Onondagas and Cayugas, and receive them into their protection upon the following conditions:

ARTICLE I

Six hostages shall be immediately delivered to the commissioners by the said nations, to remain in possession of the United States, till all the prisoners, white and black, which were taken by the said Senecas, Mohawks, Onondagas, and Cayugas, or by any of them, in the late war, from among the people of the United States, shall be delivered up.

ARTICLE II

The Oneida and Tuscarora nations shall be secured in the possession of the lands on which they are settled.

ARTICLE III

A line shall be drawn, beginning at the mouth of a creek about four miles east of Niagara, called Oyonwavea, or Johnston's Landing-Place, upon the lake named by the Indians Oswego, and by us Ontario; from thence southerly in a direction always four miles east of the carrying path, between Lake Erie and Ontario, to the mouth of Tehoseroron or Buffalo Creek on Lake Erie; thence south to the north boundary of the state of Pennsylvania; thence west to the end of the said north boundary; thence south along the west boundary of the said state, to the river Ohio; the said line from the mouth of the Oyonwayea to the Ohio, shall be the western boundary of the lands of the Six Nations, so that the Six Nations shall and do yield to the United States, all claims to the country west of the said boundary, and then they shall be secured in the peaceful possession of the lands they inhabit east and north of the same, reserving only six miles square round the fort of Oswego, to the United States, for the support of the same.

ARTICLE IV

The Commissioners of the United States, in consideration of the present circumstances of the Six Nations, and in execution of the humane and liberal views of the United States upon the signing of the above articles, will order goods to be delivered to the said Six Nations for their use and comfort. Oliver Wolcott, Richard Butler, Arthur Lee . . . Otyadonenghti, his x mark (Oneida), Dagaheari, his x mark (Oneida) . . .

Page 22: Excerpt of letter from Henry Knox to President George Washington, June 15, 1789

Transcription

In examining the question how the disturbances on the frontiers are to be quieted, two modes present themselves, by which the object might perhaps be effected; the first of which is by raising an army, and [destroying the resisting] tribes entirely, or 2ndly by forming treaties of peace with them, in which their rights and limits should be explicitly defined, and the treaties observed on the part of the United States with the most rigid justice, by punishing the whites, who should violate the same.

In considering the first mode, an inquiry would arise, whether, under the existing circumstances of affairs, the United States have a clear right, consistently with the principles of justice and the laws of nature, to proceed to the destruction or expulsion of the savages. . . . The Indians being the prior occupants, possess the right of the soil. It cannot be taken from them unless by their free consent, or by the right of conquest in case of a just war; To disposses them on any other principle, would be a gross violation of the fundamental laws of nature, and of that distributive justice which is the glory of a nation. But if it should be decided, on an abstract view of the situation, to remove by force the. . . .Indians from the territory they occupy, the finances of the United States would not at present admit. of the operation.

Page 40: Transcription of letter from Israel Chapin to Oliver Phelps on October 13, 1794

Transcription

Canandaigua, Oct. 13th, 1794

Sir

Mr. Cleveland the Bearer has rec'd of me six pound thirteen & four pence. And left your business the 30th of Sept.

The Indians are assembled here from all quarters and are in number about 1500. They behave very well yet & I hope the business will be settled to the Satisfaction of both Parties.

I have traded with a Mr. Wilder and have given 12/pn. and have taken a Deed in your name.

Your business goes on very well in this quarter and I wish you to write me every opportunity.

I am Dear Sir (in haste)
Yours Obnt [Obedient] Servant
Israel Chapin

NB Sir I have paid Mr. Cleveland two Dollars more in addition to the above L
6.13.4.

Glossary

amends Something given or done to make up for a wrong or hurt.

assimilate To take in or absorb; to adopt the cultural traditions of another group.

cession A yielding to another; a concession.

compensation Something given in payment for a loss.

concession Something given in exchange for something taken.

confederacy A united group of states or nations.

consequence An effect or result of an action.

embark To begin something new.

encroachment The taking of another's possessions or rights gradually.

fraudulent False or fake.

land speculators People who bought and sold land in high-risk situations with the hope of making a profit.

protocol A detailed plan for a procedure.

Six Nations The six Indian tribes of the Iroquois Confederacy, which included the Cayugas, Mohawks, Onondagas, Oneidas, Senecas, and Tuscaroras.

squatters People who live on land or a property that does not belong to them.

wampum Strings of beads made into belts or strands; used as money or jewelry by many Native American groups.

For More Information

WEB SITES

Due to the changing nature of Internet links, the Rosen Publishing Group, Inc., has developed an online list of Web sites related to the subject of this book. This site is updated regularly. Please use this link to access the list:

http://www.rosenlinks.com/psat/trca

For Further Reading

Englar, Mary. *The Iroquois: The Six Nations Confederacy*, New York, NY: Bridgestone Books, 2002.

Graymont, Barbara. *Indians of North America: The Iroquois*. Norman, OK: University of Oklahoma Press, 1991.

Levine, Ellen, and Shelley Hehnberger. *If You Lived with the Iroquois*. New York, NY: Scholastic Books, 1999.

Sneve, Virginia Driving Hawk, and Ronald Himlet. *The Iroquois*. New York, NY: Holiday House, 1995.

Bibliography

Campisi, Jack, and William A. Starna. "On the Road to Canandaigua: The Treaty of 1794." *American Indian Quarterly*, Fall 1995, p. 467.

Fenton, William N. *The Great Law and Longhouse: A Political History of the Iroquois Confederacy*. Norman, OK: University of Oklahoma Press, 1998.

Jemison, G. Peter, and Anna M. Schein. *Treaty of Canandaigua 1794: 200 Years of Treaty Relations between the Iroquois Confederacy and the United States*. Santa Fe, NM: Clear Light Publishers, 2000.

Jennings, Francis, ed. *The History and Culture of Iroquois Diplomacy*. Syracuse, NY: Syracuse University Press, 1985.

Johansen, Bruce Elliott, and Barbara Alice Mann. *Encyclopedia of the Haudenosaunee*. Westport, CT: Greenwood Press, 2000.

Manley, Henry S. *The Treaty of Fort Stanwix 1784*. Rome, NY: Rome Sentinel Company, 1932.

"Social Fabric." *Economist*, November 12, 1994, p. A35.

Cover: George Caitlin portrait dating from 1847–1848, *Portage Around the Falls of Niagara at Table Rock*. Part of Paul Mellon Collection.

Page 5: Hand-colored map of the Province of New York dating from 1776. Engraved by William Faden.

Page 8: *Indio, Ill with Smallpox* by unknown artist, housed in the Biblioteca del Palacio Real in Madrid, Spain.

Page 10: Part of a map dating from 1720. Image of Iroquois village in "French America." The title is *Palisaded Village*.

Page 11: Black-and-white drawing from 1570 of Atortaro, Hiawatha, and Dekanawida illustrating the founding of the Iroquois Confederacy.

Page 15: The Treaty of Fort Stanwix, October 22, 1784. Housed at the Atwater Museum in Philadelphia, Pennsylvania.

Page 18: Oil-on-canvas portrait of Arthur St. Clair executed from 1782–1784 by Charles Willson Peale.

Page 19: Black-and-white drawing of Fort Harmar created on January 1, 1789. Housed at the Hulton Archive.

Page 22: Except from Henry Knox's letter to President George Washington, written at the War Office, June 15, 1789.

Page 23: Charles Willson Peale's oil-on-canvas portrait of Henry Knox. Purchased by the City of Philadelphia at the 1854 Peale Museum sale.

Page 25: Miniature portrait of George Washington (circa 1777) by Benjamin Trott, painted on ivory. From the Musée de la Cooperation Franco-Americaine, Blerancourt, France.

Page 28: Lithograph of Cornplanter, dated 1837, by E. C. Biddle. Based on 1796 oil painting published in *The History of the Indian Tribes of North America*, by McKenney and Hall.

Page 31: Oil-on-canvas painting, *The Ohio River Near Marietta*, dated 1855, by Henry Cheever Pratt.

Page 33: Stone lithograph of Seneca war chief Red Jacket by Corbould. Image was published circa 1835 by Campbell & Burns in Philadelphia, Pennsylvania.

Page 35: A hand-colored woodcut of canoes traveling by moonlight on the Ohio River. Housed at North Wind Archives.

Page 37: Charles Willson Peale's portrait of Timothy Pickering, circa 1792–1793. Purchased by the City of Philadelphia at the 1854 Peale Museum sale.

Page 40: A letter dated October 13, 1794, written by General Israel Chapin in Canandaigua to Oliver Phelps about treaty negotiations. Housed at the Ontario County Historical Society in Canandaigua, New York.

Page 45: Proclamation of General Anthony Wayne, dated February 22, 1795. Housed at the Cincinnati Museum Center.

Page 51: Circa eighteenth-century oil-on-canvas portrait of George Washington by Joseph Wright of Derby. Housed at the Atwater Kent Museum of Philadelphia.

Page 52: The Treaty of Canandaigua, dating from 1794. One of two copies in existence, this is housed at the National Archives in Washington, D.C.

Index

ABOUT THE AUTHOR

M. G. Mateusz has graduate degrees in American and Eastern European history. He makes his home in western Nebraska with his four dogs, where he also works as a cabinetmaker. This is his first book for young readers.

PHOTO CREDITS